First published 2022

(c) 2022 Dominic Salles

All rights reserved. The right of Dominic Salles to be identified as the Author of this work has been asserted by them in accordance with the Copyright, Designs and Patents Act 1988. No part of this work may be reproduced, stored in a retrieval system, transmitted in any form or by any means, electronic, mechanical, photocopying, recording, or otherwise, without the prior permission of the Author.

Dominic Salles still lives in Swindon, with his workaholic wife Deirdre. His jiu-jitsu-loving ex-engineer son, Harry, has moved to Shoreditch and lives on the site of Shakespeare's first theatre. Destiny. For those of you who remember Bob, he is now an ex-dog.

His daughter Jess is educating students in Wales because, now Brexit is done, Brussels isn't stepping in to help the Welsh any more. She is learning to surf. He spent three months in Andorra this year, learning to snowboard. He is not as cool as he thinks.

His sister Jacey is famous for her Spanish accent, on your TV screens, and is also filming in Wales. She would be hilarious in her own YouTube channel. His 2006 Prius has just died and been rein*car*nated (who writes these puns?) as a 2019 Prius.

His YouTube channel, Mr Salles Teaches English, has reached 100,000 subscribers, about which he is childishly excited. 30% of his viewers said they improved by at least 3 grades in 2022.

Other Grade 9 Guides by Mr Salles

Language

The Mr Salles Guide to **100% at AQA GCSE English Language**
The Mr Salles Guide to **Awesome Story Writing**
The Mr Salles Quick Guide to **Awesome Description**
The Mr Salles **Ultimate Guide to Description**
The Mr Salles Quick Guide to **Grammar, Punctuation and Spelling**
The Mr Salles Ultimate Guide to **Persuasive Writing**
The Mr Salles Guide to **100% in AQA GCSE English Language Paper 1 Question 2**
The Mr Salles Guide to **100% in AQA GCSE English Language Paper 1 Question 3**
The Mr Salles Guide to **100% in AQA GCSE English Language Paper 1 Question 4**
The Mr Salles Guide to **100% in AQA GCSE English Language Paper 1 Question 5**

Literature
The Mr Salles Guide to **GCSE English Literature**
Study Guide Mr Salles Analyses **Jekyll and Hyde**
The Mr Salles Ultimate Guide to **Macbeth**
The Mr Salles Guide to **An Inspector Calls**
The Mr Salles Ultimate Guide to **A Christmas Carol**
The Mr Salles Ultimate Guide to **Romeo and Juliet**
Mr Salles **Power and Conflict** Top Grade Essay Guide (AQA Anthology): 11 Grade 9 Exam Essays!

Introduction

This guide is built round such a simple idea, that I'm shocked I never thought of it before.

The best way to understand exam answers is to read exam answers!

For each question, I want my readers to have a huge range of exam answers to past questions. You will get 24 answers, all marked to show you the full range of the mark scheme.

And I also give you my commentary for each one as to why the marks were awarded.

In real life, most of these answers would be full of spelling and punctuation errors, and still get the marks. Students who are very bad writers can still get good grades. But I've made sure that the spelling and punctuation is correct, so you can focus precisely on the exam skills of each question.

I've also rewritten each answer so that they actually make sense, and so that the students who wrote them wouldn't recognise them. I've changed most words, so 'green' becomes 'red', 'he' becomes 'she', 'fast' becomes 'quick' etc. It means the skills, sentences, detail and type of vocabulary is exactly the same as the actual students used, while nearly all the individual words are changed.

How to Use This Guide

All the answers are based on actual exam papers, which you can download from the AQA website. For copyright reasons, I can't give you the actual quotations from the exam paper. But I have rewritten these so that it will be easy for you to match up each answer with the right exam paper.

However, the guide will work brilliantly on its own, without the exam papers if you prefer.

1. Any time you sit any exam question, put your answer alongside this guide. Ask yourself, "which answer in the guide looks most like my answer?"

2. This will give you a very good guide as to what mark your answer would get.

3. Then read my commentary underneath.

4. This will tell you the sorts of things you are probably doing wrong.

5. Now, read the answers that scored more than this. Build up an idea of what gets more marks. This is even more valuable than my examiner's comments. But, you should read those too, because they teach you everything you need to know.

6. Now, write your answer again, without looking at the guide. This is the *only* way for you to work out if your exam skills are improving. If you answer a *different* question from a different paper, you won't know if you miss marks because you haven't understood the text properly, or because of a lack of exam technique.

7. **After** you have practised exam technique a couple of times, then you should try a *new* exam paper. This will measure how much improvement you have actually made, and tell you what mark you are likely to get if you took the GCSE now.

Introduction to Question 4

This question is fantastically easy. It has taken me a lot of time writing exam answers to realise this. In the past I've been guilty of overcomplicating a method for my students, even though I always tried to keep everything as simple as possible. Let's put that right here.

It's going to be simple.

Question 4 is easy because you are basically asked to give and prove your opinion about a character. I mean, if I did this with Love Island, a Harry Potter film, or any film or TV series you enjoy, you would easily give me some strong opinions with examples showing why I should agree. It's no different here.

So, what makes the question seem hard?

1. Students think it will be hard to find examples and so waste time thinking. Don't think. Writing is thinking. Just write. If you write a bad idea, you don't even have to cross it out (though I would). The examiner will just pretend anything wrong isn't actually there. No, really, they are trained just to mark the good stuff and ignore anything rubbish or wrong.

2. Students worry about the terminology to use and look for examples of simile, metaphor, alliteration, sibilance, etc, rather than just quoting stuff that backs up their opinion. Just quote. If you don't know the name if the technique, just call it **imagery**.

3. Students don't evaluate – they just state their opinion without using words which show that other interpretations and opinions might also be right. As you can see below, if you don't evaluate, you can't even get a grade 4. Just use *implies, suggests, probably, however, perhaps, might, may.* Those words evaluate for you.

4. Students forget that there are **two** opinions in the question, so they have to deal with **both**.

Mark Scheme

1. **Perceptive, detailed evaluation 16-20 marks**
2. **Clear, relevant evaluation 11-15 marks**
3. **Some evaluation 6-10 marks**
4. **Some limited comment 1-5 marks**

Problems with the Mark Scheme

Different teachers and examiners will give you totally different answers to:

- What is the difference between 'clear evaluation' and 'detailed evaluation'?
- How many evaluative points lift the answer to more than 'some evaluation'?
- How many evaluations mean the answer is 'detailed evaluation'?
- What does evaluation mean?

This is so subjective that trained examiners are allowed to disagree by up to 4 marks. This is appalling, because 4 marks is more than a grade!

So, I need to give you a method which leaves no doubt what your grade is. It will help every teacher and examiner award pretty much the same mark to the same answer. Here it is.

The Mr Salles Method

1. **State whether or not you agree with the statement.** (It is easiest to mostly agree)*.
2. **Give 20 explanations** which show how the examples make us think or feel or predict that the statement is mostly correct.
3. **Give up to 20 examples.** (Often you will be able to give more than one explanation from one quotation, so you can get away with far fewer examples).
4. **Write each example and explanation in one sentence**, not a PEE paragraph. PEE paragraphs stop you giving enough explanations and getting enough points. They take too long.
5. **Just say what the writer is doing.** Only name a technique if you know it. "Imagery" or "emphasises" scores just as highly as "imperative verb" or "asyndetic list". You don't need to be fancy, just make sense. You **don't** need to go looking for techniques, as everything will be "imagery" or used to "emphasise". And the same, bog standard techniques will always come up, "simile, metaphor, personification, alliteration and sibilance".
6. **Use words like perhaps, might, could, may, however** to show that you are evaluating.

*Later on you will see that only partially agreeing makes it easy to get extra marks, *even if you don't have enough points.*

We can summarise the method in one sentence:

Write 20 points, including *words like* **perhaps, might, could, may, however** to explain what **each one** makes us think, feel or predict.

(You will notice others in bold italic which also evaluate, but these are the main ones).

When You Read the Student Exam Answers

You will notice that I lay out each answer as numbered bullet points.

You don't have to write your exam answers this way. However, if you did, you would help the examiner. They would easily be able to see how many quotations you are using, how many points you are making, and how many explanations you are giving about what we think, feel or predict.

But it will also make **your** task easier. You will write less, and still get the marks. You will know when you have written a full mark answer. This is especially useful in your exam practice and revision.

Many of you will find that you can write more than 20 of these points in 30 minutes. That's fine – sometimes you might write a point which doesn't score, so having more than 20 is a good insurance.

But never go over your time limit! (You have 30 minutes to read the question and the extract and write your answer).

Others of you will be saying, "Wait, what, I have to write 20 points, my handwriting is not fast enough." Well, there's a solution to that. Practise writing more quickly. You don't have to be smart to be quick. But you can make yourself smart by practising.

What do Students Score on this Question Normally?

So, it's a 20 mark question. The first few marks are therefore easy to get. You might expect that no student is going to score 0-2 marks on this question, unless they are actively trying to fail the exam. So, let's split the remaining marks and assume that the average student would get 50% of them. That would give them a score of 11 marks.

Nationally, the average score on the description and narrative question is 12.3, which is out of 24. So, our prediction of 11 marks as a national average for question 4 is reasonable.

But no, the average score is in fact only 9.7, less than 50%!

This is proof that students simply don't write enough.

AQA, very unhelpfully, don't give many examples of full mark answers, perhaps because students just don't get full marks. They simply don't have the writing speed.

In my school, the highest mark for grade 9 students was 17. (Just to let you know, I don't teach in my school!) That is also the highest marked answer AQA provides for 2 of the 3 exam papers in this guide.

Consequently, I have had to write my own full mark answers for you here.

What have you learned? Jot anything here, as your revision notes.

Adapted From Language Paper 1 June 2019

Question 4

Focus this part of your answer on the second part of the source, from **line 32 to the end**.

A student said, 'This part of the story, where Albert has to find the shark which fell off the trawler and rows back with it, reveals Hardstop's cruelty. This means that we entirely sympathise with Albert.'

To what extent do you agree?

In your response, you could:

- consider whether Albert is treated with cruelty by Hardstop
- evaluate how the writer creates sympathy for Albert
- support your response with references to the text.

Response 1

1. I think that Hardstop should have got out of the trawler himself.

2. Forcing a young boy into the sea is cruel.

3. So is shouting at him and making him scared.

4. Making him go out in the gale was unfair.

5. Hardstop is nasty.

6. The rain hits him in the face and the winds push him with force.

3 marks

My Commentary

a) What is the simplest way we can work out the marks here? The easiest way to think about this is that a quotation, with an explanation linked back to the question is worth one mark.
b) An explanation on its own is worth half a mark.
c) A quotation on its own is worth half a mark.
d) A reference to the text (instead of a quotation) is worth half a mark.
e) Let's see if this actually works.
f) The student has 5 explanations in points 1-5, and one quotation in point 6. So, 6 half marks which adds up to 3 marks.
g) Notice that the student has ignored the opinion about the reader being entirely sympathetic to Albert (so they are only answering half of the question).

h) Some limited comment 1-5 marks

What have you learned? Jot anything here, as your revision notes.

Response 2

1. I completely agree that Hardstop treats Albert cruelly.

2. He sends Albert out in the storm.

3. He doesn't have anything to keep him warm, not even a coat.

4. Then he sails away and leaves Albert.

5. Albert has to follow the trawler on his own.

6. He is thin.

7. It is the middle of the night.

8. When he says "just" a shark, Hardstop gets angry with him.

9. People will have sympathy for Albert *because he doesn't fight back.*

10. *He has hidden his emotions and accepted it for a long time.*

6 marks

My Commentary

a) The student has set out their viewpoint at the start in point 1. This doesn't get any marks on its own.
b) They have made 9 points to support this view.
c) Points 9 and 10 give references to the text **and** explanations of how we feel sympathy, so score a mark each. (The reference to the text for point 10 is in point 9).
d) Points 2-8 give examples of things which indicate that Hardstop is cruel, or that we sympathise with Albert. But there is no explanation for how or why these suggest his cruelty, or cause us to feel sympathetic. So all these points only score half a mark each.
e) This gives us a total of 5.5 marks.
f) As you know, half marks can't be given. So the examiner has had to make a choice between 5 and 6.
g) When we look at points 9 and 10, we can see that this works as "some evaluation", so the answer gets 6 marks instead of 5.
h) Now we know that dealing with the second opinion in the question helps us to evaluate.
i) **Some evaluation 6-10 marks**

What have you learned? Jot anything here, as your revision notes.
_____
_____
_____
_____

Response 3

1. Hardstop treats Albert cruelly.

2. The storm is described using pathetic fallacy.

3. He can barely see *because of the power and aggression of the sea which* "pummelled and smacked his boat, spraying painfully in his face".

4. The writer evokes sympathy *because Hardstop makes Albert search in this frightening and severe weather.*

5. The description "slumped" also implies how exhausted Albert is, *which reveals Hardstop's cruelty.*

6. In addition, "Hardstop suddenly yelled at him" *which suggests a cruel and harsh tone.*

7. Albert is only trying to do his best, but Hardstop does not appreciate his effort.

8. Furthermore, the exclamation mark reveals Hardstop's anger *and suggests he is shouting loudly.*

9. His aggression towards Albert *is revealed in the instruction* "Earn your keep! Get rowing. Get rowing."

10. *We feel sympathy for Albert as he does not deserve this treatment.*

8 marks

My Commentary

a) The student states their point of view in point 1, which on its own doesn't score any marks.
b) Points 2 and 7 don't include an explanation. So they score half a mark each, giving us 1 mark in total.
c) The remaining 7 points all have a reference to the text **and** an explanation, so all score 1 mark each, giving a total of 7 marks.
d) The final total is therefore 8 marks.
e) Notice that they have spent points 1-9 on the first half of the question, but they have only given one explanation for the opinion about sympathy.
f) **Some evaluation 6-10 marks**

What have you learned? Jot anything here, as your revision notes.

9

Response 4

1. I mostly agree with this statement because, from line 32 to the end, Hardstop is cruel and domineering to Albert.

2. Firstly, Hardstop is strict and domineering, *which is revealed in the imperative* "Take it and find the shark, before it sinks".

3. **Perhaps** *he believes that the value of the shark is higher than the importance of Albert's safety*

4. **Perhaps** *ordering Albert into the incessant rain, rather than go himself, reveals that Hardstop is not manly.*

5. In addition, the verb "yelled" *reveals Hardstop's lack of control and his anger.*

6. This **perhaps** *suggests that he is so poor that the loss of the shark could damage the survival of his family.*

7. **However**, we feel sympathy for Albert *as he must row alone in the darkness and rain.*

8. *He appears to accept this.*

9. The use of violent verbs like "pummelled" and "smacked" *also makes us sympathetic.*

10. *These two verbs portray the wind as overpowering and cruel.*

11. *They suggest Albert may be too weak to cope.*

12. The use of short sentences at the end *also suggests Hardstop's cruelty.*

13. *This explains why Albert makes no response.*

12 marks

My Commentary

a) The student sets out a qualified view of the statement (this means they partially agree, or partially disagree). This tells the examiner that they are going to evaluate why they mostly, but not totally, agree.
b) Although this partial agreement doesn't get a mark on its own, it means the examiner already wants to give it at least 11 marks (as that is where 'clear ... evaluation' starts).
c) The next 12 points all include a reference to the text *and* an explanation, so score 1 mark each.
d) Using words like 'perhaps' and 'however' also helps the examiner see that the student is evaluating.
e) **Clear, relevant evaluation 11-15 marks**

Response 5

1. I *partially agree* that Hardstop's sudden abandonment of Albert reveals his cruel nature.

2. The writer uses a pattern of short sentences: "We'll wait at Smuggler's Point. Find us there. Bring back the shark." *This abruptness reveals Hardstop's impatience.*

3. *This suggests he wants to leave Albert.*

4. *This neglect and mistreatment of Albert makes us feel sympathy for him.*

5. The description of the poor weather conditions *also suggest Hardstop's cruelty.*

6. *These also invite our sympathy for Albert.*

7. We are made to feel protective and sympathetic towards Albert *through the imagery of "pummelled and smacked" which describes the wind's violence.*

8. *Albert has a stoic acceptance* of the rain and Hardstop's instructions.

9. *This* **could** *imply that Albert is used to the harshness of Hardstop's words.*

10. *It also implies he is used to the harshness of his treatment in poor weather.*

11. We feel sympathy for him *as we realise Albert* **may** *have experienced much pain and struggle.*

12. *Our sympathy is increased here because of his youth.*

13. **However,** *Hardstop may not be an entirely cruel character, as his cruelty* **might** *be caused by his failing business,* **so I partially disagree with the statement**.

14. His repetition of "just" in response to his cabin boy: "Just? How dare you tell me 'just'?" **could** *suggest he is trying to teach him that each catch is critical to the business.*

15. *This is probably because of their financial situation.*

16. *This* **might** *make us understand Hardstop's circumstances and help us feel sympathy for him.*

17. To conclude, Hardstop is a mostly cruel character, *yet this* **might** *be explained by the stress of his circumstances.*

15 marks

My Commentary

a) We can see that the answer fulfils the four elements of structuring an answer that the examiner wants:
   1. Outline a partial agreement with the statement at the beginning.
   2. Use 'however' or another connective which shows your partial disagreement.
   3. Use words like perhaps, may, could, probably etc to show that you are evaluating.
   4. Finish with a concluding sentence.

b) However, at its simplest, the student makes 17 points.
c) Points 1 and 17 are the introduction and conclusion, which score no marks on their own (although they are helpful to prove that the answer is an evaluation).
d) The remaining 15 points all include a reference to the text and an explanation, so the answer scores 15 marks.
e) It might seem a bit harsh that 15 points does not count as detailed, but that's exams for you. Points make prizes.
f) **Clear, relevant evaluation 11-15 marks**

What have you learned? Jot anything here, as your revision notes.

Response 6

1. Hardstop's treatment of Albert clearly shows a lack of care for his cabin boy, *so we feel sympathy for him.*

2. He leaves Albert in pouring rain and darkness, *which would **probably** make the experience terrifying.*

3. *This is **probably** made worse because he is young, alone and in a stormy sea.*

4. The writer also invokes sympathy for Albert in his description of the weather *because he has to face the full force of the wind without support*, as "each wave pummelled and smacked his boat, spraying spitefully in his face".

5. Moreover, "pummelled" and "smacked" *convey the power of the rain and waves, and imply Albert **must have** struggled in it.*

6. This is conveyed most powerfully by "smacked" *which we associate with actions taken in rage and anger.*

7. In addition, we feel sympathy *because Albert is stoic and brave, coping on his own despite the harsh conditions and treatment.*

8. *His isolation makes us feel both protective and sympathetic towards Albert, as though we might help him feel less alone.*

9. *This reveals Hardstop's cruelty to Albert because a captain's role is to look after the safety of the crew and the welfare of his young cabin boy doing an adult job.*

10. *This cruelty is emphasised* when Hardstop remains in the waterproof and warm trawler, enjoying the comfort of dry seats.

11. *This contrast makes us feel increasing sympathy for Albert.*

12. *It also makes us despise Hardstop for his treatment of young Albert.*

13. **However,** the writer hints at Hardstop's poverty, *which **might** suggest that Hardstop's actions aren't entirely cruel.*

14. The narrative is set in the 1930s, where poverty was more common, and when children were expected to work to help their families.

15. Hardstop **probably** works the hardest to support his family, so sending Albert out alone in the rain and darkness is **not necessarily** cruel.

16. Albert **might** simply be carrying out his role in the crew, and *Hardstop **may** be desperate not to lose valuable goods which can be sold for profit.*

17. *This desperation is suggested by his instruction,* "Don't just sit there. Earn your keep! Get rowing. Get rowing. See who wants to buy fresh shark meat. Shift those oars!".

18. *We sense both his urgency and that he has only the best intentions in earning enough to pay his crew.*

19. In conclusion, we can see Hardstop lacks compassion for his cabin boy. ***Although*** *he desires to look after his business, he acts cruelly towards Albert.*

20. He refuses to empathise with Albert's feelings of isolation in being left alone in the darkness and rain at sea, *and this creates our sympathy for him.*

18 marks

(A good writer would be able to combine several points into one sentence. For example, point 3 could easily be included in point 2. Points 11, 12 and 13 could easily be shortened and combined. However, I have set it out this way so that you can clearly see the different points the student is making).

My Commentary

a) We can see 5 easy steps to full marks:
   1. Write an introductory sentence which suggests whether you agree or partially agree.
   2. Mostly agree with the statement.
   3. Introduce your partial disagreement with 'however'.
   4. Use the words ***might, may, could, probably, however, although, probably*** (and any other evaluative words) as frequently as possible to show you are evaluating.
   5. Write a conclusion.
   6. Write 20 explanations to get 20 marks.

b) Points 1 and 20 act as an introduction and a conclusion, to prove the answer is evaluative.

c) The remaining 18 points all include an explanation which refers back to the ideas of cruelty or sympathy in the question. So it scores 18 marks.

d) Points make prizes. Going into detail about one quotation is not as useful as having two developed points about two different quotations or two different references to the text. Quotes make prizes.

e) This student is clearly a better student of English than the student who wrote the answer coming up next which scored full marks. Why? They just made more points.

f) **Perceptive, detailed evaluation 16-20 marks**

What have you learned? Jot anything here, as your revision notes.

_____
_____
_____
_____
_____
_____
_____
_____

Response 7

1. I agree that Albert's captain treats him with cruelty and rudeness.

2. *His cruelty is shown when* he sends Albert out in the rain and the storm, and then sails away, leaving him.

3. The imagery to describe this "into the darkening storm" *also creates a suggestion of evil.*

4. *His **possible** neglect is emphasised when* "To Albert the trawler seemed to glide away. In the squall and hail he watched the orange glow of the cabin gradually disappear", *as it accentuates the abandonment.*

5. **We get a sense** *that Albert watches this painful abandonment through the phrase "glide away" which implies that it takes a long time.*

6. *This implies Hardstop's cruelty in going away from Albert slowly, forcing him to watch the trawler leave.*

7. *We feel sympathetic when* the waves "pummelled and smacked his boat, spraying spitefully in his face".

8. *This hyperbole emphasises his suffering and pain.*

9. *The onomatopoeia of "smacked" also emphasises the hyperbolic power of the waves **as though** it is literally pounding him.*

10. *The personification of "spraying spitefully"* **might** *also suggest that these are a reflection of Albert's own feelings at being crushed by his captain's actions.*

11. *The choice of verb "pummelled" also **hints** that **perhaps** Hardstop's cruel treatment at other times includes physical abuse, which increases our sympathy.*

12. *The use of "sudden" in* "He wiped the torrent from his eyes and was rewarded with a sudden dancing glow of house lights" *suggests that Albert is also looking for a change in the way he is treated, inviting out sympathy.*

13. *The metaphor of "dancing glow" also implies that he has felt abandoned in the sea and is now excited at the thought of human company suggested by the "house lights".*

14. *This description also works metaphorically, implying the "torrent from his eyes"* **may** *represent his tears and sadness at the way Hardstop has treated him.*

15. This contrasts with the quickness of "dancing glow" which is emphasised with the word "rewarded". *It suggests that Albert hopes for change, that life might improve.*

16. *We also feel this longing for change when* he sees the "house lights".

17. *We feel sympathy for Albert, as we wonder what he is trying to escape from to attain the happiness which is suggested by* the imagery of "dancing".

18. Finally, the writer uses dialogue *to reveal Hardstop's cruelty.*

19. So "Albert sat in silence, slumped over the oars" *which implies that he is afraid to voice his thoughts to his captain.*

20. *This is confirmed when* "Hardstop yelled" and Albert responds immediately to his tone and authority.

21. "Albert complied immediately", *which suggests he is used to being mistreated by Hardstop.*

22. In conclusion, *we also have the impression that Albert accepts Hardstop's mistreatment because it is a recurring experience for him. This again makes us feel sympathetic.*

20 marks

My Commentary

The full mark answer takes the simplest approach possible: easy steps to full marks:

1. Simply agree with the statement.
2. Make as many points as you can, dealing with as many quotations as you can, in your time limit.
3. Use the words **might, may, could, probably, however, although, probably** (and any other evaluative words) as frequently as possible to show you are evaluating.
4. Write a conclusion.

   a) An even simpler way of looking at this is that every '*implies*' or '*suggests*' is also evaluative, because it does not say the interpretation is certain.
   b) The student has an introduction and conclusion which don't directly score marks. The conclusion reminds the examiner that the answer is evaluative. The introduction and conclusion are points 1 and 22.
   c) The student writes 20 explanations about the quotations and references to the text, and therefore gets 20 marks.
   d) This answer shows the value of exam technique in this question. I would argue that the student who wrote the 18 mark answer is actually a better student of English – they understand how novels work, and have a wide knowledge of history which they apply to their reading of books. Books always respond to the issues of the time in which they are written and set. But, this last student has better marks because they simply make more points about language, even though they don't consider the source of the text at all.
   e) Points make prizes.
   f) **Perceptive, detailed evaluation 16-20 marks**

What have you learned? Jot anything here, as your revision notes.

_____
_____
_____
_____

Adapted From Language Paper 1 November 2018

Question 4

Focus this part of your answer on the second part of the source from **line 29 to the end**.

A student said, 'This part of the story, where the soldiers meet the robot, shows Eugene has good reasons to run. The robot appears invincible!'

To what extent do you agree?

In your response, you could:

- consider your own impressions of Eugene's reaction to the robot
- evaluate how the writer describes the robot
- support your response with references to the text.

[20 marks]

Response 1

1. I agree with the student.

2. *Eugene is afraid and wants to turn back, as we see when* he says "we would be mad to attack, we can't get through that armour".

3. *Eugene was afraid of the robot* which intended to slaughter the soldiers.

4. The robot was "like the Titanic". *This shows how enormous it was.*

5. *Although the rest of them were brave, I think Eugene was brave for admitting he was scared.*

6. *Eugene, and indeed anyone present, would be right to run away.*

4 marks

My Commentary

a) Point 1 is an introduction without an explanation, so it doesn't score a mark.
b) Point 6 is a conclusion, which sums up points 2-5. It doesn't explain anything new, or explain another quotation. So it doesn't get a mark.
c) Points 2-5 give 4 explanations and so score 4 marks.
d) **Some limited comment 1-5 marks**

Response 2

1. I agree that the robot seems invincible.

2. The men only knew the average sizes of other mobile weapons, but not the true size of the robot. *When they saw its true size, the men were right to want to run away.*

3. *The writer emphasises how* the robot walks and the size of its thighs.

4. One of the men says, "I had no idea it would be so massive and well armoured". *This reveals that the men did not understand how large the robot was going to be.*

5. One of them says, "We can't survive this. We should pull back". *This proves that the robot is an unstoppable killing machine and these smart men realise their mistake.*

6. Eugene understood that the robot couldn't be stopped. *He therefore wanted to hide.*

7. Even though Eugene believed the robot couldn't be stopped, *he still thought it was worth a try to shoot it*: "the machine guns rattled off hundreds of rounds".

6 marks

My Commentary

a) The student has responded to the statement in point 1. This works as an introduction, but scores no marks on its own.
b) Then the student has given 6 explanations. So the answer scores 6 marks.
c) **Some evaluation 6-10 marks**

What have you learned? Jot anything here, as your revision notes.

Response 3

1. I agree with the statement.

2. The source ends with a detailed account of how powerful and terrifying the robot is. *For this reason, Eugene is right to want to run away.*

3. The writer describes the robot as terrifying and a monster. *So we believe Eugene should consider escaping as soon as they encounter the robot.*

4. But I also disagree with the student. Eugene had volunteered as an elite soldier to fight this robot, *so he clearly understood what to expect.*

5. *Consequently he is then wrong to panic when he sees the robot.*

6. *The robot is described as gigantic and terrifying.*

7. *But this shouldn't surprise* Eugene, who would know that the robot is the most fearsome mechanical weapon in history.

8. Eugene has a duty to put himself in danger as a member of this special unit. *Therefore Eugene is to blame for joining the unit to destroy the robot.*

9. So when "The robot, detecting their heat signals, plunged at them with a shriek of metal", *Eugene should not have begun to run.*

8 marks

My Commentary

a) The student has responded to the statement in point 1. This is not an explanation, so on its own it doesn't score a mark.
b) The 8 points 2-9 all include an explanation, so they score 8 marks.
c) **Some evaluation 6-10 marks**

What have you learned? Jot anything here, as your revision notes.

_____
_____
_____
_____
_____
_____
_____
_____
_____

Response 4

1. I agree with the student.

2. *In fact, I feel afraid for the soldiers when I read* the frightening description of the robot.

3. *We can see how menacing and dangerous the robot is* in the quotation, "This God of war".

4. The word "God" emphasises its power and "war" emphasises this menace.

5. *Further proof is* the simile describing its armour as *"*like the plating on some futuristic jet-fighter" *which conveys how terrifying it is.*

6. The word "futuristic" *implies that the robot is unbeatable.*

7. Eugene reacts as though he is facing an inevitable death, as are the other soldiers. *I believe we would react the same way.*

8. *The soldiers also struggle to cope with feelings of fear* in response to the robot. *Eugene reacts to their response.*

9. *Panic fills Eugene with fear, which is emphasised when* he says "Abort! Abort!".

10. *This is emphasised with* "Eugene stared helplessly at his ineffective machine gun".

11. But I also disagree with the student's statement. *The other characters showed bravery in trying to fight the robot, which we see when* "They let loose a salvo of bullets and anti-tank missiles at the pneumatic joints of the machine".

12. Following this example of bravery, *Eugene reacts with fear, saying* "this is a suicide mission. This thing won't be brought down".

13. To conclude, I mostly agree with the student *because the whole text builds suspense, building to the climax. This makes all the members of the elite unit feel afraid, and it proves how terrifying the robot is. This causes Eugene to run.*

10 marks

My Commentary

a) The student has made 13 points.
b) Point 1 responds to the statement and does not score a mark on its own.
c) Point 2 looks like an explanation, but it is in fact a summary of what the student writes in points 3-6. So point 2 is just an introduction. It doesn't make a new point, or offer a new quotation and explanation. So it scores no marks.
d) Points 3-12 all give explanations, so score 10 marks.
e) Point 13 is an evaluative conclusion, which doesn't score any marks on its own, but helps the examiner feel happy about deciding it is worth the 10 marks needed in the mark band.
f) **Some evaluation 6-10 marks**

Response 5

1. I agree with the student's statement.

2. *Eugene was right to run, as* all the soldiers collectively decide to return to their chopper rather than face the robot.

3. They decide to flee *because they believe Eugene is right to say* "It won't be put down".

4. *They also believe he is right when he observes* "We can't survive this. We should pull back".

5. *These create a sense of doubt and a crisis in self-belief. The soldiers believe it will be futile even to attempt to defeat the robot.*

6. Eugene also claims, "I've never been a coward. I've fought almost impossible odds before". *So Eugene fears he may be killed by the robot.*

7. *Eugene has never been in such a dangerous situation before, so he is right to run.*

8. I also feel that *the machine is described in ways which make us fear it,* for example, "The beak glistened, accentuating its sharp edges like a tank sized axe."

9. Focusing on the "titanium … plating" *makes us feel that the soldiers cannot possibly defeat the machine.*

10. Because "carapace" is a protective layer *we believe that they cannot even damage the robot.*

11. To conclude, *the main reason I agree with the student is that Eugene believes the robot is invincible like a* "God of war".

12. *Consequently, I agree that the robot is invincible.*

13. *Therefore Eugene has every right to panic and run.*

11 marks

My Commentary

a) The first point is simply to agree with the statement, so we know it does not score a mark.
b) That leaves 12 explanations, for a maximum of 12 marks.
c) However, point 12 sums up what the student has written before, with no new evidence or new explanation of what we are made to think, feel or predict. So it scores no marks.
d) That leaves a score of 11 marks.
e) Notice what a good writer this student is, and how clearly they understand the text. However, they can't get high marks because they haven't explained enough points.
f) Points make prizes, and every quotation allows you to make 1 or 2 points.
g) **Clear, relevant evaluation 11-15 marks**

Response 6

1. I agree with the student's statement.

2. Eugene observes that the robot "won't be brought down". *This statement also means that Eugene is right to run.*

3. The robot is also portrayed as the most advanced mechanical weapon, *which emphasises how they won't be able to destroy it.*

4. *This creates tension, as we imagine death is inevitable, either the death of one of the soldiers or **perhaps** all of them.*

5. *We also realise that their weapons are ineffective,* as Eugene observers that "even the anti-tank missiles might as well have been rubber bullets".

6. *This is emphasised when their ineffective weapons are contrasted to* the "titanium" armour of the robot.

7. *This also justifies a sense of panic, because the weapons are their best protection, and we believe they **may** do little damage to the robot.*

8. The robot is also described as a "God of war", *which implies that the robot is far more powerful than anyone on its battleground.*

9. *We have a very awe inspired view of gods and can imagine terrible things it will do to the men.*

10. In addition, the eyes of the robot are heat seeking, "detecting their heat signals". *This reveals that the robot can't be fooled by camouflage, and they cannot hide from it.*

11. *The robot is also portrayed as unstoppable in other ways,* for example repeatedly referring to the robot as "relentless".

12. *This implies that the robot **might** never run out of power or fuel.*

13. We see this in "it knows we're here!" and "it won't be put down", *which also make the robot **appear** invincible.*

14. *This relentlessness also increases a sense of fear in the men and the reader.*

13 marks

My Commentary

a) Point 1: as you know, it is very helpful for the examiner to know you are answering the question. So, beginning with your agreement or partial agreement is very helpful, even though it scores no marks on its own.
b) There are 13 explanations, so it scores 13 marks.
c) It is also worth noting that the answer uses 7 quotations – roughly two points are made for each quotation. This is a template for how to approach the question. 20 marks are easiest to achieve with 10 or more quotations.

d) You will also notice the vocabulary of evaluation this student is using, compared to the answers which scored fewer marks.
e) **Clear, relevant evaluation 11-15 marks**

What have you learned? Jot anything here, as your revision notes.

Response 7

1. I agree that Eugene is right to run because the robot is truly terrifying.

2. The simile comparing "the anti-tank launcher" to a "pea shooter" *makes the launcher **seem** useless in destroying the robot.*

3. *Consequently, when the robot does attack, Eugene's anti-tank launcher has no way of protecting him.*

4. Because Eugene has no weapon more powerful than this, *he is right to feel fear when facing the robot.*

5. The robot is also described as a gigantic and unstoppable machine.

6. So we find out it has "titanium ... plating". *This armour suggests that the robot has been equipped to defeat any attacker.*

7. *This implies the men, who have never encountered such a deadly enemy, will find it almost impossible to defeat the robot.*

8. *Consequently, Eugene should be scared. To emphasise this,* as we saw earlier, he described his launcher as a "pea shooter".

9. *To illustrate how terrifying the robot is, the writer focuses on the overall appearance of the robot,* which has "two snake-like tentacles" in addition to its head sharpened "like a tank-sized axe".

10. *These combine to imply the robot's power which make it **appear** terrifying.*

11. *Then the writer focuses on terrifying details,* such as the robot's eyes, which glow with "volcanic fires" and can easily find the soldiers with an "infrared beam".

12. *This description emphasises the robot's furious and unstoppable power.*

13. *This "expressionless" eye reveals that the robot has no fear of the soldiers.*

14. *Its focus **appears** to be entirely on killing the soldiers.*

15. The robot is continuously referred to as "relentless". *This also emphasises its lack of human weakness, as it has been designed to complete each mission.*

16. *This implies that it is a brilliantly designed and efficient killing machine which won't be deflected by the soldiers' weapons or tactics.*

17. Eugene **appears** *to understand this fully, which explains his terror at the robot's ability to kill them all if it spots them.*

18. Overall, *the robot is portrayed as petrifying* because it is described as impossible to "be put down" which shows that Eugene was right to run away as if it had attacked the men, they would have no chance against it.

19. Consequently, Eugene should be scared and run as we realise the soldiers would be unable to stop an attack from this invincible monster.

16 marks

My Commentary

a) Points 1 and 19 state the student's viewpoint and offer a conclusion. Neither of them introduce a new point or explanation, so on their own, they don't gain a mark. They do help to confirm that the answer is evaluative.
b) This leaves 17 available marks for the 17 explanations.
c) Point 3 is really a similar explanation to point 2, rather than a new explanation. So together they combine to make one mark.
d) All the other points include an explanation of the effect on the reader, so they all score a mark.
e) So the score is 16.
f) **Perceptive, detailed evaluation 16-20 marks**

What have you learned? Jot anything here, as your revision notes.

Response 8

1. I agree with the student's statement.

2. Firstly, the writer describes the robot as like a monster.

3. The robot is also described as a "a massive, malignant deity".

4. This also <u>emphasises</u> the robot's great power as similar to the power of a god.

5. Viewing it as a "deity" also <u>suggests</u> that this monster has instantly replaced the character's faith in their own religion and god.

6. The monster's appearance is so terrifying that they instantly decide their own god cannot protect them from the robot's power.

7. Consequently, Eugene's first reaction is to conclude that the robot "won't be put down".

8. This <u>implies</u> that the robot is so terrifying that he cannot put his fear into words.

9. Before he saw the robot, Eugene boasted about all the battles he had fought in: "of Orwell, of Wuthering Heights, Silas and Marner". This <u>implies</u> that he is a man who is normally unafraid of any enemy.

10. Because he is described as a great soldier we know he is not easily frightened.

11. So we know his terror of the robot must be very real.

12. His reaction to the robot also *reveals that the robot is terrifying and other-worldly.*

13. The monster is also referred to as "This God of war". Like a "god" we **imagine** the robot can conquer vast areas of land and rule over them easily.

14. It also <u>suggests</u> that the robot will stop at nothing to defend its kingdom, even killing the soldiers.

15. Just this quotation on its own *reveals the robot's enormous unstoppable power.*

16. Consequently, any man would feel terror and want to run because they could be killed easily by this gigantic machine.

17. And this also <u>suggests</u> that the robot is invincible.

18. Therefore, Eugene is right to run away from the robot.

17 marks

My Commentary

a) The student sets out their point of view in point 1.
b) The remaining 17 points can all score 1 mark each, because they all include an explanation.

c) The answer uses only 5 quotations, which I think is cutting it a bit fine. It is easier to get the marks by using more quotations.
d) Another high risk the student has taken is in not using obviously evaluative language. But, this does highlight how important *implies, suggests* and *emphasises* are. I've underlined them in this answer so that you can see the impact.
e) However, the examiner has to think about the overall quality of the answer, in particular points 4 and 5 and 9 and 10 which other students do not typically pick up on. But you can't be sure of spotting things others won't. It is much safer to simply give more examples.
f) Anyway, points make prizes. 17 explained points gain 17 marks.
g) **Perceptive, detailed evaluation 16-20 marks**

What have you learned? Jot anything here, as your revision notes.

My Response

1. I partially agree with the student's statement.

2. *Eugene **may** be wrong to feel fear when he says*, "It won't be put down", *and his fear **may** be unjustified.*

3. However, his reaction is to speak "calmly" *which suggests that his fear **may not** be the result of panic, but of correctly assessing the danger.*

4. He realises that their weapons are going to be useless against the robot, noting that "The anti-tank grenade launcher…might as well be a pea shooter".

5. This leads him to conclude that "This is a suicide mission". *Soldiers are used to risking their lives, but here Eugene feels he has no hope of survival which **must be** terrifying.*

6. But Eugene is also a trained soldier, *and he **should not** let his fear turn to panic.*

7. Consequently, when Tarquin orders "Silence soldier", *we can see that Eugene is **probably** endangering the lives of the others.*

8. *Tarquin's reaction also suggests that he clearly believes Eugene's reaction is very wrong*: "We don't carry cowards in this unit".

9. However, *Eugene's reaction suggests that he **may not** be panicking. Instead he is trying to save the unit, instead of them all going* "home in a body bag".

10. Other soldiers notice that the robot can detect their "body heat", *which means that they can't hide from it, and can't launch a surprise attack. This confirms that Eugene's fears are logical.*

11. The robot is described as "This God of war", *which suggests that it is all powerful and cannot be destroyed, certainly not by mere men.*

12. *It is **even more** dangerous an enemy when we find that* "Even its armour was a weapon", harnessing the energy of the sun.

13. The armour is "boiling the air", *so **we can imagine** even getting close to the robot is going to lead to certain death.*

14. Eugene is **probably** going against his order when he demands "Abort! Abort!", but he makes clear this is not cowardice: "I've never been a coward". *This implies he is right to want to run.*

15. He also assess the chance of surviving the robot as being "impossible odds", *which sounds logical, because he lists other terrifying threats which he has overcome in battle.*

16. When he tells the men "We're outgunned, we all know it", *none of the other soldiers disagree with him, which implies that he is right.*

17. However, the reaction of the other men, and of Tarquin, *suggests that even if Eugene is right about the impossibility of defeating the robot, he is wrong to try to survive instead.* They all refuse to run. In fact, Tarquin even tells him to do the opposite, "Walk slowly".

18. Ironically, once Eugene starts to run, he attracts the robot's attention and puts them all at risk, *so running was exactly the wrong thing to do*: "You've made us a target!"

19. *The description of the battle does suggest that Eugene was right to think that the robot was invincible.* "They let loose a salvo of bullets and anti-tank missiles", but it seems to have no effect on the robot.

20. They are even aiming for its most vulnerable parts, the "pneumatic joints", *but they **appear** to have no effect.*

21. The robot's lasers are described as "burning out a cancer". *This suggests that the robot will stop at nothing.*

22. *However, we all know that cancers are notoriously difficult to stop, which introduces a moment of hope, that the men **might** still find a way to defeat the robot.*

23. The battle leads to the men being moments away from death, "broken, but not yet dead". *This implies that, when they defeat the robot, they are incredibly lucky.*

24. Tarquin orders all his men to fire at "the eye", which appears to disable the robot, as it falls to the ground. *This suggests that Eugene **should** instead have followed orders, and risked his life against impossible odds.*

25. *However, the ending also implies how unlikely this victory is. It is just as rare as the sinking of* "the Titanic", or finding "Atlantis".

26. Comparing the Robot to these also emphasises how massive it is. *This suggests that it is therefore invincible.*

27. *However, we also know that in the case of both the Titanic and Atlantic, the opposite is true. This implies that Eugene was wrong to run, and the robot was never invincible.*

20 marks

My Commentary

a) This is longer than you would need to get full marks.
b) However, you can see that simply writing about things you spot moving through the text, line by line, will mean that you will find plenty to write about.
c) I've also tried to show you that the evidence is not going to be really difficult to find. Almost every line will have something you could comment on.

d) Point 1 simply states a partial agreement, to remind me to evaluate. It doesn't score any marks on its own.
e) That leaves us with 26 points, which all include an explanation. So, they would all score marks. You can get full marks combining any 20 of those 26.
f) Tactically I would make at least one point about the ending, just to show the examiner that you are considering all of the lines referred to in the question.

What have you learned? Jot anything here, as your revision notes.

Adapted From Language Paper 1 November 2020

Question 4

Focus this part of your answer on the second part of the source, from **line 23 to the end**.

A student said, "the disappearance of the giant hound was not a surprise. The writer made it obvious that Robert had imagined the dog, so it was never there."

To what extent do you agree?

In your response, you could:

- consider the disappearance of the giant hound
- evaluate how the writer presents the giant hound
- support your response with references to the text.

[20 marks]

Response 1

1. I agree *the dog is produced by Robert's imagination. We can see this at the end* "But when he reached the field, the giant hound was nowhere to be seen."

2. Robert had been looking at the dog and then grabbed his shoes "quickly" but in that time the dog had disappeared. *How did it disappear so quickly?*

3. *Another reason which suggests it is an imaginary dog is the unusual description*, "had a bizarre coat: a skin dappled in grey and blue, and splotches of white, like a child's painting".

4. But *I also disagree that it is an imaginary dog. Before this, Lara also saw the dog*, "Lara appeared to ignore this hound and carried on searching for butterflies".

4 marks

My Commentary

The student has given 4 points and 4 explanations. So the answer scores 4 marks.

What have you learned? Jot anything here, as your revision notes.

_____
_____
_____
_____

Response 2

1. I can only partially agree with the student's statement.

2. The text includes clues that *the dog **could be** both imaginary and real.*

3. *The other children are not worried about the dog's appearance*, but just carry on playing.

4. We can see this in the quote, "Lara appeared to ignore this hound and carried on searching for butterflies." *This reveals that Lara **might** not actually be able to see the dog.*

5. *This suggests that the dog is imaginary.*

6. *Or **perhaps** not.*

6 marks

My Commentary

a) The examiner's comments here help us realise that the Mr Salles Method is not perfect. Dammit! Yes, at the lower end of the mark scheme, it is even easier to get marks than my method.
b) You just have to partially agree with the statement and use evaluative words.
c) So, when we read the answer, there are clearly only 4 explanations, in points 2-5. I would only give this 4 marks. (In fact, the student who wrote Response 1 seems to me a better student than this one).
d) But in points 1, 2 and 6 the student points out that there is evidence that the dog **could** be real or imaginary.
e) So, the examiner says, "hey, look, this student is clearly **evaluating**, because they are aware that the dog may or may not be real".
f) This is terrible news for me. I hate the fact that the marks are this easy to get, and that I am not 100% right! Never mind, I will get over it. No, really, I'm fine. I'm just crying with happiness because of the good news.
g) Yes the good news is that saying why you partially agree, and why there is evidence for both agreeing and disagreeing with the statement gets you extra marks.
h) The good news is that using ***might, perhaps*** and ***could*** is enough to show that you are evaluating.
i) But the other good news is that my method would still get you the marks.
j) **Some evaluation 6-10 marks**

What have you learned? Jot anything here, as your revision notes.

_____
_____
_____
_____
_____
_____

Response 3

1. I agree with the student's statement.

2. "Lara appeared to ignore this hound and carried on searching for butterflies". *If the dog was actually real Lara would react to it.*

3. *She would wonder why she had never seen it before.*

4. *She would be scared by its massive size.*

5. **Perhaps** only Robert can see the hound because "He noticed that the doll looked very much like Lara".

6. This **might** mean that he is just imagining threats to his daughter.

7. This **might** suggest that Robert spent his childhood in a similar house to this and is being reminded of his own childhood.

8. **Perhaps** Robert is dreaming, or imagining the dog, which is suggested by "There was something unlikely about the way it moved: slow, like an old man or a grandfather on a rocking chair".

9. This suggests that the dog is not real.

8 marks

My Commentary

a) Point 1 states the student's point of view, but doesn't include an explanation, so doesn't score any marks.
b) Points 2-9 all include an explanation, so each one scores a mark, giving 8 marks.
c) **Some evaluation 6-10 marks**

What have you learned? Jot anything here, as your revision notes.

Response 4

1. I definitely agree that the dog is simply part of Robert's imagination.

2. *We can see that the dog's movement is described in a very unlikely way like a person* "There was something unlikely about the way it moved: slow, like an old man or a grandfather on a rocking chair".

3. The dog is described as a "grandfather" and filling the children with "confidence" *which is much more like a real person than a dog.*

4. *It is impossible for a dog to fill a* "child with confidence" *through its calmness, which* suggests *that the dog is part of Robert's imagination.*

5. In addition, I definitely agree with the statement *because Lara did not react to the huge dog and so she has not even noticed it.*

6. *We can see this when* "Lara appeared to ignore this hound and carried on searching for butterflies."

7. The word "appeared" suggests *that Lara doesn't choose to ignore the dog, she doesn't see it because it isn't there.*

8. *This* emphasises *that Lara doesn't see the dog because Robert is imagining it.*

9. However, there are reasons to disagree with the statement. *Robert* **may** *actually be seeing a supernatural dog, a ghost who lives in the field.*

10. *This can be seen in the mystery of how it got into the field, over such a high wall,* "It was high, much too high even for this beast to jump, surely."

11. The dog also appeared just as the children went out to play *which* implies *it simply wanted to play with them.*

10 marks

My Commentary

a) Point 1 gives a point of view about the statement, but does not include an explanation, so scores no marks.
b) Points 2-11 all include an explanation, so they all score 1 mark each.
c) We can see that **suggests, implies** and **emphasises** are also treated as evaluative words. I've underlined them in this answer.
d) **Some evaluation 6-10 marks**

Response 5

1. I both disagree and agree with the student's statement.

2. Because the focus changes from the dog, then to the field, then back to the dog, *we **might** imagine anything could have happened in between.*

3. *We can imagine that Robert's mental health is affected badly when,* "He relaxed, grateful for this chance to recover from the anxieties of the last week. He shut his eyes".

4. Although I don't agree that he is imagining the dog, the word "anxieties" *does suggest that Robert **might** be suffering some sort of trauma.*

5. *This **might** justify the student's opinion that the dog is imaginary.*

6. *However, to counter this, is the detailed description of the dog,* "It wore a red, studded collar and had a bizarre coat: a skin dappled in grey and blue, and splotches of white, like a child's painting". *This detail suggests that the dog is very real.*

7. Describing the dog's "anxious expression" and its feelings *also implies that Robert is seeing something real.*

8. Robert notices *the dog has other emotions too,* "The hound stole a glance at the house, a sudden, secretive check, as though scared of seeing someone in the upstairs windows watching."

9. *This action suggests that the dog is scared of someone in the house.*

10. *But **perhaps** these anxieties are just brought on by the "anxieties" Robert himself is feeling.*

11. *In addition, each description of the dog makes it **appear** mysterious, which suggests the student is right.*

12. *The human characteristics of the dog are also odd,* "Something was definitely odd about it. Robert had seen wisdom in the hound's anxious glance".

13. *The word "wisdom" is very unlike any dog, which also hints that it **could** be a supernatural figure.*

14. *Or the unlikeliness **could** suggest that the dog must be imaginary.*

12 marks

My Commentary

a) The student has made 14 points.
b) The first point is a reaction to the statement, but does not include an explanation, so it scores no marks.
c) Points 2-14 all include explanations, so should score 13 marks.
d) So, which one is a 'pretend' explanation?
e) Point 2. Yes, anything might have happened while Robert was looking at the children and then the field. But this doesn't help us decide whether the dog is real or imaginary unless

the student deliberately tells us. E.g. "while Robert was looking elsewhere it is very possible that a dog entered the field". This would be a "clear" explanation. So, point 2 scores no marks.

f) **Clear, relevant evaluation 11-15 marks**

What have you learned? Jot anything here, as your revision notes.

Response 6

1. I partly agree with the statement *as the dog is described as an imaginary character*. It "had a bizarre coat: a skin dappled in grey and blue, and splotches of white, like a child's painting".

2. *We **can infer** from this that, like a painting, the dog **could** be a figure from make believe.*

3. The "bizarre" description of the dog's colours *also suggests that the dog **could** be magical, like a Disney cartoon come to life.*

4. The dog is compared to a grandfather, "like an old man or a grandfather on a rocking chair, a calm, constant presence that fills a child with confidence." *This **seems** very unlikely.*

5. *It also suggests that Robert is over imaginative.*

6. *We can also see that his imagination is too powerful* when "Robert had seen wisdom in the hound's anxious glance" *which **seems** too human to be a description of a real dog.*

7. *We can also imagine that the dog is supernatural because his children don't **seem** to notice the huge dog.*

8. *Or this **could** mean that the dog is just a part of Robert's imagination.*

9. "The hound stole a glance at the house, a sudden, secretive check, as though scared of seeing someone in the upstairs windows watching", *which suggests that the dog is too human to be a real dog.*

10. Also the "wisdom in the hound's anxious glance" *is too intelligent for a dog, which makes us **think** that the dog is not really there.*

11. Robert notices that the dog is chewing a rag doll that "looked very much like Lara". *This suggests that the dog is just a projection of Robert's fears for his daughter.*

12. The sudden disappearance of the dog, "the giant hound was nowhere to be seen" *also suggests that the dog was never there.*

13. Robert tried to move quickly to put on his shoes but the dog still vanished in that time. *This makes Robert wonder if the dog was ever **even** there.*

13 marks

My Commentary

a) There are 13 explanations and so there are 13 marks!
b) **Clear, relevant evaluation 11-15 marks**

Response 7

1. I agree with the statement because the disappearance of the dog is not a surprise.

2. One reason for this is *that the dog did not want to be seen, so* "The hound stole a glance at the house, a sudden, secretive check".

3. *We can also infer that the dog **may** be a ghost because of Lara's lack of reaction to its enormous size,* "Lara appeared to ignore this hound and carried on searching for butterflies".

4. *We also get the **impression** that the hound is trying to make itself invisible as it* "also looked hunched".

5. *These details make the reader **predict** that the dog will disappear when* Robert takes his eyes off it as he gets his shoes on.

6. Furthermore, the dog is described "There was something unlikely about the way it moved" and it had "wisdom" in its expression. *This suggests that this is not a normal dog.*

7. It makes us curious about how the dog can have such a human intelligence.

8. When the dog makes a "secretive check, as though scared of seeing someone in the upstairs windows watching" *we can see that it is using its intelligence to avoid being seen.*

9. Because the wall "was high, much too high even for this beast to jump" *we **imagine** a supernatural reason for the dog to appear.*

10. *This makes us **predict** that the dog would also disappear.*

11. *The writer also makes sure that the dog reproduces the same emotions as Robert.* This is why the dog is both "anxious" and "hunched" which is just like the "anxiety" Robert felt at the beginning.

12. *This suggests that the student **could** be right that the dog is imagined by Robert.*

13. *The writer also makes a comparison between the dog's rag doll and Lara which helps explain why the dog disappears.*

14. Because the wall is so tall *we **can infer** that there was no way for the dog to escape. This suggests that the dog must have been a ghost.*

15. *This also explains why Lara doesn't seem afraid of the dog.*

16. *The descriptions which make the dog seem too human also suggest that it is not real and **could** be supernatural.* For example it has "a calm, constant presence that fills a child with confidence", is like a "grandfather" and has a look of "wisdom".

17. The disappearance of the dog is also not a surprise, *because it was obviously scared of being seen.*

18. In conclusion, the fact that it could not jump over the wall shows us that the dog is also supernatural.

15 marks

My Commentary

a) The student has make 18 points, but point 1 just comments on the statement without an explanation, and point 18 just repeats earlier points as a conclusion. So these points get no marks.
b) This leaves 16 points which all include an explanation. So, which one is a 'pretend' explanation?
c) Point 13 is totally unclear. We have no idea why the similarity of the rag doll to Lara means the dog is likely to disappear. So this gets no marks.

1. **Clear, relevant evaluation 11-15 marks**

What have you learned? Jot anything here, as your revision notes.

Response 8

1. I agree with the student that the disappearance of the dog is not a surprise.

2. This is because of the narrative structure. The dog is not properly described until the middle of the extract. *This distances it from the children and Robert.*

3. Calling it a "black beast" *also makes us **question whether** it is a real dog.*

4. The word "beast" *also implies that it **might** be more than a dog, perhaps supernatural.*

5. The hound's presence in the walled field ***seems*** *unlikely.*

6. On the other hand, the fact that this is a dog and not another character ***could*** *mean that its appearance is not going to be important to the plot.*

7. Therefore this ***could*** *be the reason that the writer makes the dog disappear.*

8. In addition, the detail that the dog held a doll that "looked very much like Lara" *suggests that Robert is letting his imagination influence what he is actually seeing.*

9. *It is very unlikely that the rag doll would look like Robert's daughter.*

10. Conversely, describing the dog as a "hound" and a "beast" *reminds us of evil.*

11. *This reminds us of how animals are described in supernatural stories.*

12. *It implies that the dog is not just supernatural, but sinister.*

13. *This idea is emphasised through* the "rag doll" *which we **might** associate with how actions performed on a voodoo doll affect the person the doll represents.*

14. Alternatively, the doll's resemblance to Lara ***could*** *reveal Robert's concern for his daughter and his suppressed fears about the dangers she will face growing up.*

15. Or ***perhaps*** *he is simply imagining that his children won't enjoy their childhood innocence for much longer.*

16. *This makes us **question** the origin of the "mastiff".*

17. *We therefore question **whether** it real.*

18. When Robert notices "the dog's anxious expression", *we **can infer** that he is simply transferring his own feelings of anxiety onto an imaginary presence or being.*

19. Consequently, Robert tries to rid himself of this anxiety by projecting onto the dog.

20. On the other hand, the "anxiety" felt by the dog ***could*** *foreshadow sinister events which are about to occur.*

21. This makes us wonder about the dog's true nature and worry about what will happen to the family in later chapters.

17 marks

My Commentary

a) This is a student who is clearly writing enough to get full marks, and certainly has the understanding to do so.
b) But the answer will also help you see how easy it is to write points which don't answer the question.
c) Point 1 gets no marks, because it does not include an explanation.
d) Point 2 is correct, but it does not actually explain why this means that the dog is not real or will disappear. So it doesn't score a mark, it isn't answering the question.
e) Points 6 and 7 are the opposite of the right answer! No writer ever includes a character and then thinks, nah, they're not important, I'll make them disappear! They just edit them out so that they never appeared in the first place. So, these are two explanations which score no marks. To be fair, the student realises this, and keeps plugging away with answers that do make sense.
f) All the other points include an explanation, so they all score a mark each. So, 17 marks.
g) **Perceptive, detailed evaluation 16-20 marks**

What have you learned? Jot anything here, as your revision notes.

My Response

1. I mostly agree with the student's statement.

2. Describing the dog as "a black beast" *rather than a dog suggests that it is an imaginary character.*

3. *Although the dog feels real to Robert,* he feels it is chewing something which "might be a rag doll". *This implies that **even he is not sure** if he should trust his vision.*

4. Next Lara "appeared to ignore this hound" even though Robert sees it as a "beast". *This implies that it is **very unlikely** that the dog is actually there, as Lara couldn't be expected to ignore it **if it were** real.*

5. *The physical description of the dog also makes it **appear** unrealistic, like a cartoon, or a* "child's painting".

6. *This **appears to be a strong hint** that the dog is a figment of his imagination.*

7. *Robert also **can't be sure** that the dog is real, because he is looking through a stained glass window and therefore looks for a* "clearer pane".

8. *We can **infer** that the dog is produced by Robert's fear and earlier* "anxieties" *because he immediately imagines that it is* "ready to strike".

9. *Another clue that this is **probably** his imagination is what happens in reality.* The dog doesn't actually strike and his children are unharmed.

10. *His own thoughts also imply that it might be impossible for such a huge dog to climb the fence into the field,* "It was high, much too high even for this beast to jump, surely."

11. *The dog also **seems** to reflect Robert's own feelings of anxiety,* so he noticed "the dog's anxious expression".

12. *This implies it is **probably** a projection of his own fears for his children.*

13. The dog is also playing with "a rag doll", *which is also **unlikely** and therefore **probably** imaginary.*

14. The description that the doll looks "very much like Lara" *also implies that this is a projection of Robert's fears, rather than a real dog chewing on a real doll.*

15. *The dog also **appears** to leave the doll intact,* even though Robert sees that it has "glistening fangs", *whereas such a dog, if real, would **probably** destroy it.*

16. *The writer points this out that instead of terrifying a child through its giant appearance, it has a* "presence that fills a child with confidence". *This **appears** unlikely.*

17. *This continues with the **unlikely** idea that* the dog has "wisdom". *These descriptions are much **more like** a human than a real dog.*

18. *This does open up an **alternative** idea, that the dog **may** be supernatural. This **would** explain* its strange intelligence, and its ability to suddenly appear.

19. The convention that not all the characters can see a ghost is also well known in literature, at least since the ghosts in A Christmas Carol.

20. The dog vanishes in the short time between Robert seeing it and going outside. *The speed of this suggests that it was never **actually** there.*

21. However, this fact *backs up both interpretations, meaning that the dog **may** be an imaginary embodiment of his fears, or **may** be a supernatural presence.*

My Commentary

a) Point 1 states a partial agreement, but scores no marks on its own.
b) Points 2-21 all include an explanation, and all score 1 mark each.
c) Exam boards are supposed to ensure that each question has the same level of difficulty each year. Yet I could not easily find more points to add to this answer. It suggests that this is a harder question to get full marks in than other papers.

What have you learned? Jot anything here, as your revision notes.

Printed in Great Britain
by Amazon